SEW YOUR OWN
FELT ADVENT CALENDAR

First published in 2018

Search Press Limited
Wellwood, North Farm Road,
Tunbridge Wells, Kent TN2 3DR

Photographs by Paul Bricknell at Search Press Studios

ISBN: 978-1-78221-491-5

Suppliers

If you have difficulty in obtaining any of the materials and
equipment mentioned in this book, then please visit the
Search Press website for details of suppliers:
www.searchpress.com

You are invited to view the author's work at:
etsy.com/shop/sachiyoishii
visit her website at: knitsbysachi.com
visit her blog at: knitsbysachi.wordpress.com
search for KnitsbySachi on www.ravelry.com
or search for Knits by Sachi on Facebook

Acknowledgements

I would like to thank everyone in the Search
Press team, especially Katie French and
Sophie Kersey, for helping me create such a
wonderful book. I would also like to thank the
designers, Juan Hayward and Emma Sutcliffe,
for the beautiful layout, and the photographer,
Paul Bricknell, for the photography. Thanks also
go to Clover Mfg Co. Ltd for supplying tools.

Printed in China through Asia Pacific Offset

SEW YOUR OWN
FELT ADVENT CALENDAR

WITH 24 MINI FELT TOYS TO MAKE FOR CHRISTMAS

SACHIYO ISHII

SEARCH PRESS

CONTENTS

THE TOYS 20

INTRODUCTION

Every year in November, my sister-in-law sends us an advent calendar from Tokyo. It is one of the highlights of the festive season and we always look forward to it. The calendar is made by a renowned chocolatier, with delightful illustrations on the box featuring little Christmas elves in red and green. Each window contains a variety of individually wrapped chocolates and occasionally you find little toys – a wonderful surprise! My children take turns savouring the chocolates while I hang the toys on our tree. We now have a nice collection of toys from the calendars.

I was introduced to advent calendars quite late in life. They did not exist when I was growing up in Japan. It is a charming idea to reveal a small treat on each day of December leading up to Christmas Eve. I would certainly have loved it as a child.

So, with the patterns in this book, I am making up for the joy I missed by having fun creating my own. Calendars come in a multitude of forms, from simple paper ones with flaps to painted wooden boxes. I wanted to make something simple and reusable with materials that are easily obtainable. The prospect of making as many as twenty-four toys was very exciting.

And what a lot of fun I had as I drew illustrations and designed toys, then decorated, stitched and stuffed! Felt is very easy to handle and soon I had more than enough items to fill all the pockets of the calendar.

I have collected the ideas to share with you here. You do not need to be an expert at sewing. The methods are straightforward and can be enjoyed by people of all skill levels.

There is also plenty of room for you to explore. Add ribbons, bells, beads or other embellishments. Use felts with glitter or patterns. If you want to change the size of a toy, simply enlarge or reduce the template. The toys can also be used as lovely gifts or stocking fillers.

Plan ahead to bring out the calendar on the first day of December or enjoy making one item each day up to Christmas Eve. Perhaps make it into a collective effort with school or charity members – what a perfect way to get together and celebrate the festive season.

Happy sewing and Merry Christmas!

MATERIALS & TOOLS

FELT

There are different kinds of felt sheets on the market: synthetic, synthetic and wool mix and pure wool. Pure wool is always nice and soft to the touch but it is not an absolute requirement for this book. However, don't choose a loosely woven fabric or your seams may come apart. You need only small amounts for the toys, so they can be made with felt squares. The calendar itself requires fairly large pieces, so purchase felt sold by the metre (yard) for this.

THREAD

Sewing thread

You can use all-purpose sewing thread to sew the felt pieces together. Thread can be cotton or polyester.

Yarn

For embroidery on felt, I have used fingering (4-ply) yarn. You can also use embroidery thread.

Tacking/basting thread

You need tacking/basting thread to make the calendar pockets.

Embroidery thread

I have attached size 05 pearl cotton embroidery thread to some of the items to make a hanging loop, but you can use any thread, yarn or cord.

STUFFING

Polyester toy stuffing is used for most of the projects. For the Gingerbread man, I have used thick cardboard to create a flat biscuit-like appearance. You can use toy stuffing for the project if you wish.

FOAM BOARD

I have used 5mm (1/8in) thick, A2 size (42 x 59.4cm/16½ x 23½in) foam board to support the calendar. You could use cardboard, but it needs to be thick and sturdy. The cardboard may bend after it is enclosed in the felt fabric.

Alternatively, you can make the calendar without board and use it like a tapestry. This type is less sturdy, but on the plus side it can be folded and stored away when not in use.

OTHER MATERIALS

You will also need small bells, ribbons and glue.

TOOLS

Pens to mark fabric

I use ballpoint pen for most fabric, but air erasable pen is best for writing on white fabric and white charcoal pencil for black.

Tracing paper and pencil

For transferring the designs to make paper templates.

Sewing needles

I use ordinary sewing needles, a blunt darning needle and a sharp-pointed chenille needle with a large eye to embroider eyes and noses and sew on hair.

Fabric, thread and paper scissors

Remember never to cut paper with your good fabric scissors or it will blunt them.

Ruler and tape measure

You will need these for measuring and for cutting straight lines.

Sewing machine

This is for sewing the calendar itself. You can hand sew this if you prefer.

Bamboo chopstick

This is an amazingly useful tool. Turn the fabric inside out and, aided by a chopstick, you can push small parts right out to the edge. You can also use it to help you stuff dolls and animals.

Crochet hook

You only need a crochet hook if you decide to crochet the Angel toy's halo. You can achieve a similar result using chain stitch.

Clockwise from top right: fabric scissors, ballpoint pen, air erasable pen, white charcoal pencil, pencil, crochet hook, tape measure, sewing needles, tracing paper, chopsticks, ruler and scissors for paper and thread.

MAKING THE CALENDAR

Materials

Cream felt, sold as
150cm (59in) widths;
90cm (35½in)

5mm (⅛in) thick A2 size
white foam board (see
page 8)

Felt for numbers,
5 x 17cm (2 x 6¾in)
in yellow-green, pink,
yellow, lilac, sky-blue
or any colour of
your choice

Cotton thread; cream and
colours to match your
felt numbers

Tacking (basting) thread

Sewing machine
(optional)

Size

43 x 61cm (17 x 24in)

Pocket, cut 24

1 Cut out twenty-four
pockets in cream felt,
using the template
left. Use the number
templates on page 14
to cut out numbers in
different colours of felt.

2 Fold the pockets at
the fold lines and tack/
baste in place.

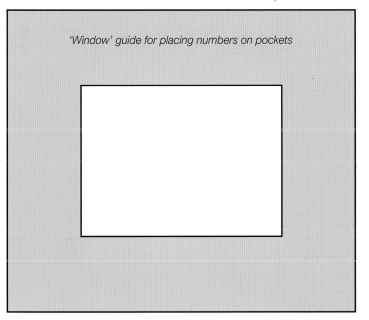

'Window' guide for placing numbers on pockets

3 Machine sew or hand back stitch each pocket at the sides and bottom edge. Make discreet hand stitches to secure the inner flaps.

4 Use the template left to make a card 'window' to help you to place the numbers centrally on the pockets.

Number templates

1 2 3 4
5 6 7 8
9 0

5 Sew the numbers on to the pockets with overcast stitches, using matching thread.

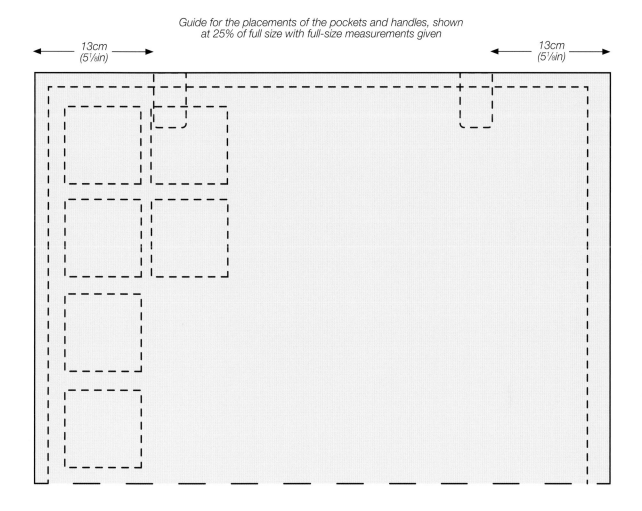

Guide for the placements of the pockets and handles, shown at 25% of full size with full-size measurements given

13cm (5⅛in)

13cm (5⅛in)

6 Cut the main calendar piece from cream felt to 87 x 63cm (34¼ x 24¾in) and mark the centre of the length with pins. Arrange the prepared pockets evenly on the top half of the piece. Start as shown above and continue, placing all twenty-four. Hand stitch the pockets in place, first with tacking/ basting thread and then with sewing thread.

Sewing guide for the calendar, shown at 25% of full size, with full-size measurements given

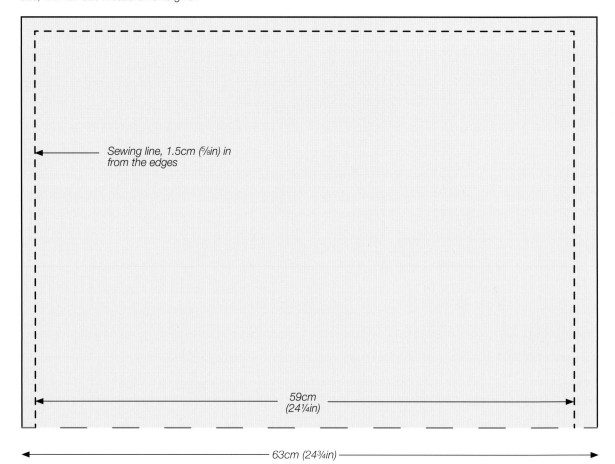

Sewing line, 1.5cm (⅝in) in from the edges

59cm (24¼in)

63cm (24¾in)

7 Cut out the handle pieces in cream felt using the template (opposite). Fold in half lengthwise and sew the side edges together with cream thread and blanket stitches. Repeat for the other piece.

Handles, cut 2

8 Remove the tacking/basting and the marking pins and fold the bottom half of the calendar over the top half, covering the pockets. Fold the handles in half horizontally, sandwich them between the top and bottom panels and secure with pins. Sew round 1.5cm (⅝in) from the edge with the wrong side out (preferably with a sewing machine), leaving one of the side edges open to insert the foam board.

9 Turn the work right side out. Insert the board, fold in the sewing allowance and hand stitch to close, using ladder stitch.

The completed calendar.

The toys

BASIC TECHNIQUES

Using the templates

A bold line is the cutting line, a dotted line is the sewing line and a red dotted line is the fold line. A dotted line is also used at times to show how the piece fits onto another piece.

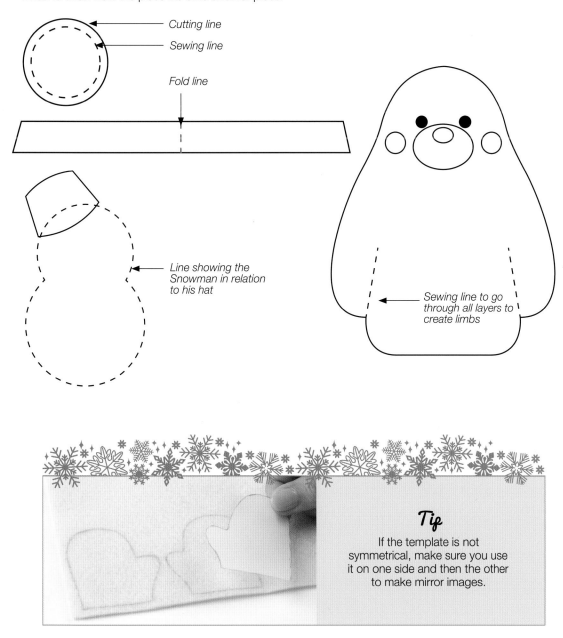

Cutting line

Sewing line

Fold line

Line showing the Snowman in relation to his hat

Sewing line to go through all layers to create limbs

Tip

If the template is not symmetrical, make sure you use it on one side and then the other to make mirror images.

Blanket stitch

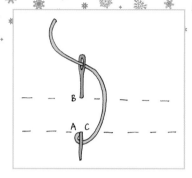 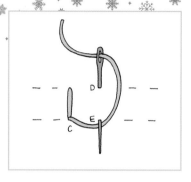 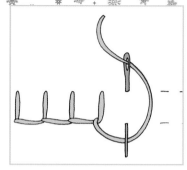

1 Bring the needle up at A and insert it at B to make a loop. Bring it through at C, inside the loop and right beside where you first came up. Pull the thread through.

2 Insert the needle at D, creating a loop, and bring it through at E, inside the loop.

3 Continue in this way.

Chain stitch

This is used for the Angel's halo (page 59).

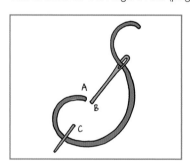 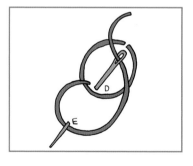 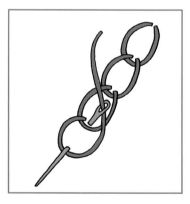

1 Bring the needle up through the fabric at A and pull the thread through. Insert the needle at B, as close as possible to A, and bring it up at C. Keep the thread under the needle. Pull the thread through gently to form the first chain.

2 Insert the needle at D, as close as possible to C, and bring the needle up at E. Keeping the thread under the needle, pull the thread through gently to form the second chain.

3 Continue in this way, making evenly sized chain stitches, until the line of stitching is complete.

French knot

These are used for eyes and noses. Take the needle through the yarn, separating the fibres, instead of taking the needle out between the stitches. This prevents the features from sinking into the face.

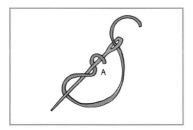

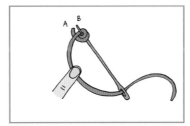

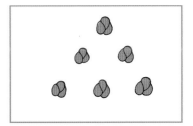

1 Bring the thread through where the knot is required at A. Holding the thread between your thumb and finger, wrap it round the needle twice.

2 Hold the thread firmly with your thumb and turn the needle back to A. Insert it as close to A as possible, at B, and pull the thread through to form a knot.

3 To hide the yarn end when you have finished making French knots for eyes and noses, take the needle out at the back of the head, then stitch into the head and trim the end.

Fly stitch

This is used for the Owl's eyes and feathers (page 46).

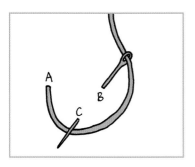

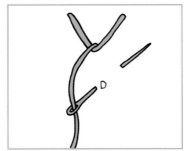

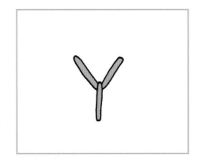

1 Bring the needle up at A and take it down at B, leaving a loop of thread. Come up at C inside the loop.

2 Take the needle down at D, just below C but on the outside of the loop, to complete the first stitch.

The finished stitch.

Tip

If the toy is embroidered, complete the embroidery first before sewing the main pieces together using blanket stitch.

GLOVE

Materials

To make one blue glove:

White felt, 7 x 10cm (2¾ x 4in)

Lilac felt, 3 x 3cm (1⅛ x 1⅛in)

Sky-blue felt, 2 x 2cm (¾ x ¾in) and
    1 x 9cm (⅜ x 3½in)

Cotton thread in white, lilac and sky-blue

Small amount of lilac and sky-blue fingering
    (4-ply) yarn or embroidery thread

Size

7cm (2¾in) long

Glove, cut 2

Hearts, cut 1 of each

Cuff, cut 1

1 Use the templates to cut out the glove pieces in white felt and the hearts in lilac and sky-blue. Attach the smaller heart to the bigger one with sky-blue thread and overcast stitches.

2 Attach the bigger heart to the front panel of the glove with lilac thread and overcast stitches.

3 Embroider the pattern shown below with lilac fingering (4-ply) yarn or embroidery thread.

4 Sew the front and back glove pieces together with sky-blue fingering (4-ply) yarn or embroidery thread, using blanket stitches.

5 Cut out the cuff in blue felt. Attach it to the glove base with sky-blue thread and blanket stitches.

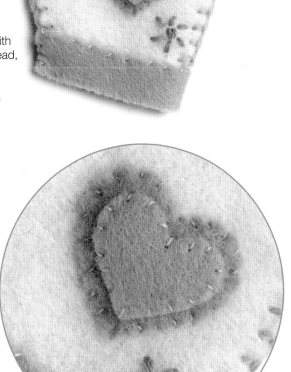

The glove made in pink

POINSETTIA

Materials

Red felt, 10 x 20cm (4 x 8in)

Yellow-green felt, 2.5 x 2.5cm (1 x 1in)

Cream felt, 1 x 23cm (⅜ x 9in)

Cotton thread in red, yellow and green

Brooch pin (optional)

Size

8cm (3⅛in)

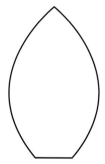

Large petal, cut 10

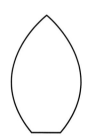

Small petal, cut 10

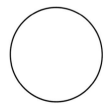

Back, cut 1

Strip for centre. Place dotted line on fold of fabric to double length

1 Use the templates to cut out large and small petals in red felt. Sew the edges of the petals with red thread and blanket stitches.

2 Use the template to cut out a strip of cream felt for the centre. Fold it seven times to make the central stamens of the flower.

3 Tie the ends together firmly with cream thread.

4 Sew the smaller petals together at the centre, insert the stamens and secure with stitches.

5 Connect the larger petals at the centre in the same way and attach them to back of the smaller petals.

6 Use the template to cut out the back in green felt and attach it with yellow-green thread and overcast stitches to hide the centre. Attach a brooch pin if desired.

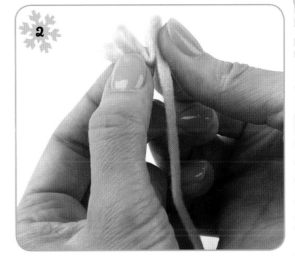

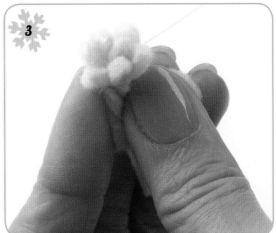

CHRISTMAS TREE

Materials

Green felt, 6 x 10cm (2⅜ x 4in)

Brown felt, 3 x 3cm (1⅛ x 1⅛in)

Small amounts of sky-blue, red, pink, lilac, yellow-green, white and yellow felt

Cotton threads to match felt colours

0.5cm (¼in) bell

Toy stuffing

Small amount of pink pearl cotton size 05 embroidery thread

Size

8cm (3⅛in) high

Star, cut 2

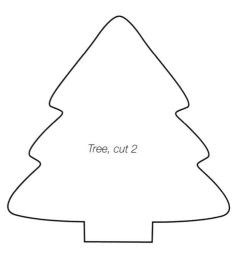

Tree, cut 2

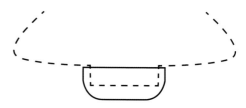

Trunk, cut 2. Dotted line shows position of tree

Large bauble, cut 3

Medium bauble, cut 2

Small bauble, cut 3

1 Use the templates to cut two tree pieces in green felt and baubles in various colours and sizes. Attach the baubles to the front tree piece with overcast stitches and matching threads.

2 With green cotton thread, sew the front and back tree pieces together with blanket stitches. Leave the base open.

3 Stuff the tree. Use the template to cut two trunk pieces in brown felt. Sandwich the tree base between the trunk pieces and sew the trunk edges with brown thread and blanket stitches. Insert small amount of stuffing into the trunk before closing if preferred.

4 Use the template to cut two star pieces in yellow felt. Sandwich the top of the tree between the star pieces and blanket stitch with yellow thread to secure the star.

5 Thread the bell onto embroidery thread and attach it to tree. The thread makes a hanging loop.

Tip

If you find sewing on baubles fiddly, glue them on after all sewing is finished as for the Holly Wreath.

CANDY CANE

Materials

To make one:

White felt, 6 x 9cm (2⅜ x 3½in)

Red felt, 3 x 6cm (1⅛ x 2⅜in) for berries and 0.8 x 24cm (¼ x 9½in) strip for body

Green felt, 5 x 5cm (2 x 2in)

Cotton thread in red, white and yellow

Gold ribbon, 12cm (4¾in)

Toy stuffing

Glue

Size

8cm (3⅛in)

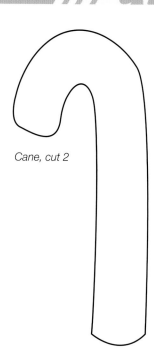

Cane, cut 2

Berries, cut 2

Holly leaves, cut 4

Red stripe. Place the dotted line on the fold of the fabric to double the length

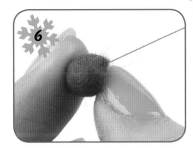

1 Use the template to cut two canes in white felt. Sew them together with white thread and blanket stitches. Insert stuffing as you sew.

2 Use the template to cut the stripe from red felt. Wrap the cane with the stripe and secure it at the edges with red thread and overcast stitches.

3 Using the template, cut four holly leaves from green felt and glue them together in pairs. Attach the leaves to the candy cane.

4 Use the template to cut two holly berry pieces in red felt. Sew running stitch round the edge of one.

5 Push in a little stuffing with the end of a chopstick.

6 Pull the thread tight to close the berry and secure with stitches. Make a second berry and attach both to the candy cane.

7 Tie the gold ribbon in a bow and secure it with a few stitches, using yellow thread.

RABBIT

Materials

White felt, 10 x 10cm (4 x 4in)

Fair skin-colour felt, 2 x 2cm (¾ x ¾in)

Pale pink felt, 2 x 2cm (¾ x ¾in)

Rust felt, 1 x 1cm (⅜ x ⅜in)

Brown felt, 0.5 x 0.5cm (¼ x ¼in)

Cotton thread in white or pale pink, rust and fair skin-colour

Small amount of dark brown fingering (4-ply) yarn

Toy stuffing

Size

9.5cm (3¾in)

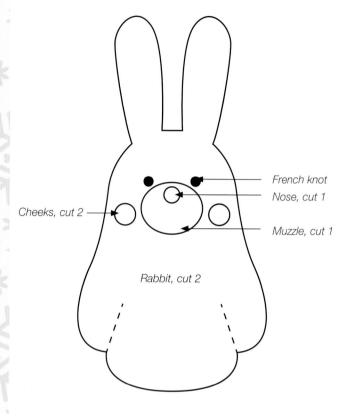

French knot

Nose, cut 1

Cheeks, cut 2

Muzzle, cut 1

Rabbit, cut 2

Pads, cut 6

Feet, cut 2

1 Use the templates to cut out two rabbits in white felt and a muzzle piece in fair skin-colour felt. Sew the muzzle to the face of one rabbit piece, using fair skin-colour thread and overcast stitches.

2 Use the template to cut cheeks from rust felt and attach them to the face using rust thread and overcast stitches.

3 Use the template to cut feet and pads from pale pink felt and attach paw to the rabbit front using pale pink thread and overcast stitches.

4 Cut a nose from brown felt and attach it to the muzzle using brown thread and overcast stitches.

5 Starting with one side of the bottom edge, sew the rabbit together using white thread and blanket stitches. Leave the bottom edge open.

6 Stuff the body and close the bottom edge.

7 With white thread, pierce the body with back stitches where indicated with dotted lines in template, to make the front legs.

BROWN BEAR

Materials

Brown felt, 10 x 10cm (4 x 4in)

Fair skin-colour felt, 2 x 2cm (¾ x ¾in)

Pale pink felt, 2 x 2cm (¾ x ¾in)

Pink felt, 1 x 1cm (⅜ x ⅜in)

Cotton thread in brown, fair skin-colour, pale pink and pink

Toy stuffing

Size

8cm (3⅛in)

Ear, cut 2

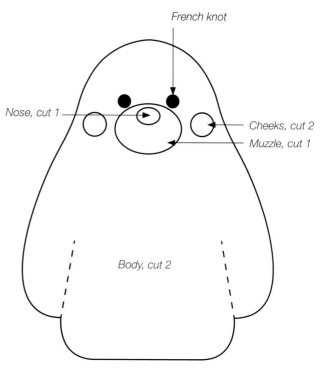

French knot

Nose, cut 1

Cheeks, cut 2

Muzzle, cut 1

Body, cut 2

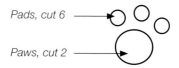

Pads, cut 6

Paws, cut 2

1 Use the template to cut two body pieces from brown felt and a muzzle from fair skin-colour felt. Attach the muzzle to the face using fair skin-colour thread and overcast stitches.

2 Cut two cheeks from pink felt and attach to the face using pink thread and overcast stitches.

3 Use the template to cut two paws and six pads from pale pink felt and attach to the body using pale pink thread and overcast stitches.

4 Cut a nose from brown felt and attach to the muzzle using brown thread and overcast stitches.

5 Starting with one side of bottom edge, sew the body pieces together, using brown thread and blanket stitches. Cut two ears from brown felt. Insert them as shown between the body pieces and continue stitching the body to secure the ears. Blanket stitch all round, leaving the bottom edge open.

6 Stuff the body and close the bottom.

7 With brown thread, pierce the body with back stitches where indicated by dotted lines in the template, to create the front legs.

ROBIN

Materials

To make one robin:

Brown felt, 5 x 10cm (2 x 4in)

Grey felt, 4 x 5cm (1½ x 2in)

Red felt, 2 x 3cm (¾ x 1⅛in)

Small amounts of pink and yellow felt

Small amount of black fingering (4-ply) yarn or embroidery thread

Cotton thread in brown, grey, pink, yellow and red

Toy stuffing

Size

5cm (2in) wide

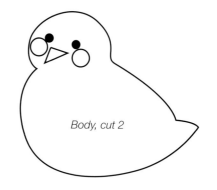

Body, cut 2

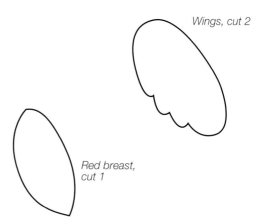

Wings, cut 2

Red breast,
cut 1

1 Use the templates to cut two body pieces from brown felt, two cheeks from pink felt and a beak from yellow felt. Attach the cheeks and beak to the face with overcast stitches using matching thread. With black fingering (4-ply) yarn, French knot the eyes.

2 Use the template to cut a breast piece from red felt and sew its inner edge to the body with red thread and overcast stitches.

3 Blanket stitch all round the two body pieces with brown thread and stuff the body. Use red thread for the breast piece, piercing through all three layers.

4 Use the template to cut two wings in grey felt. Sandwich the body between the wings and stitch the wings at the upper edge with grey thread and blanket stitches. Attach the other edges of the wings to the body with overcast stitches.

Robin, back view

37

ELF

Materials

Green felt, 6 x 8cm (2⅜ x 3⅛in)

Fair skin-colour felt, 5 x 5cm (2 x 2in)

Brown felt, 2 x 5cm (¾ x 2in)

Yellow felt, 2 x 6cm (¾ x 2⅜in)

Cotton thread in fair skin-colour, brown, green and yellow

Toy stuffing

Small amount of dark brown and fair skin-colour fingering (4-ply) yarn or embroidery thread

Glue

Size

9cm (3½in)

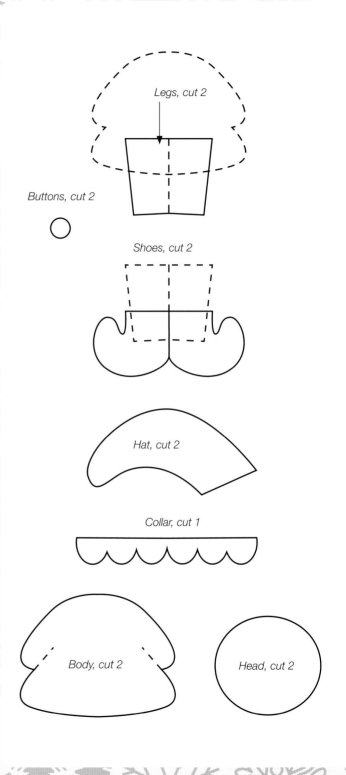

Legs, cut 2

Buttons, cut 2

Shoes, cut 2

Hat, cut 2

Collar, cut 1

Body, cut 2

Head, cut 2

1 Use the legs template to cut two pieces of felt in fair skin-colour felt. Place one on top of the other. Sew up the side edges with fair skin-colour thread and blanket stitches. Leave the top and bottom edges open.

2 Cut two shoe pieces from brown felt. Sandwich the legs with the shoe pieces, covering two-thirds of the leg length. Sew the shoe pieces together with brown thread and blanket stitches.

3 Insert stuffing from the top of the legs. Pierce through the centre of the shoes with brown thread and backstitch to separate the shoes. With fair skin-colour thread, pierce through the centre of the leg with backstitch to separate the legs.

4 Use the template to cut two body pieces in green felt. Sandwich the legs between the pieces as shown. Sew up the bottom of the body pieces with green thread and overcast stitches to secure the legs.

5 Sew round the rest of the body with blanket stitches, stuffing it as you go. With green thread, pierce through the body where indicated in dotted lines to create the arms.

6 Use the template to cut two head pieces in fair skin-colour felt. With fingering (4-ply) fair skin-colour yarn or embroidery thread, French knot the nose on the face. With fingering (4-ply) dark brown yarn or embroidery thread, French knot the eyes.

7 Sew the embroidered face piece to the other head piece with fair skin-colour thread and blanket stitches, stuffing the head as you go.

8 Use the template to cut two hat pieces in green felt. With green thread, blanket stitch the pieces together, leaving the bottom edge open. Insert the head and attach it to the hat with overcast stitches.

9 Attach the head to the body using ladder stitch (see the Angel on page 59). Use the templates to cut a collar piece and two buttons in yellow felt. Attach the collar to the neck, stitching at the back of the neck with yellow thread. Glue on the buttons.

SQUIRREL

Materials

Brown felt, 8 x 8cm (3⅛ x 3⅛in)

Cream felt, 2 x 2cm (¾ x ¾in)

Red felt, 0.5 x 7cm (¼ x 2¾in)

Small amount of pink felt

Cotton thread in brown, pink and cream

Small amount of dark brown fingering
  (4-ply) yarn or embroidery thread

Toy stuffing

Size

5cm (2in)

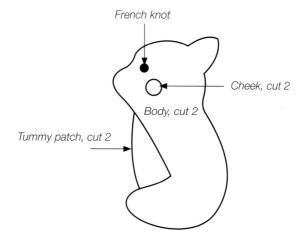

French knot

Cheek, cut 2

Body, cut 2

Tummy patch, cut 2

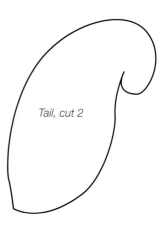

Tail, cut 2

Paws, cut 2

Scarf, cut 1

1 Use the templates to cut two body pieces and two tail pieces in brown felt and two tummy patches in cream felt. Cut two cheek circles in pink felt. Work on each body piece as follows, to make the two mirror-image sides: attach the tummy patch to the body with cream thread and overcast stitches. Attach the cheek circles with pink thread and overcast stitches. With fingering (4-ply) dark brown yarn or embroidery thread, French knot an eye.

2 Sew the two body pieces together with brown thread and blanket stitches. Stuff the body as you go. Use the template to cut out two paws from brown felt. Attach them to the body with brown thread and overcast stitches.

3 Use the template to cut out two tail pieces in brown felt and sew them together with brown thread and blanket stitches, stuffing as you go.

4 Attach the tail to the body with ladder stitches. Cut out a scarf in red felt and tie it round the neck.

 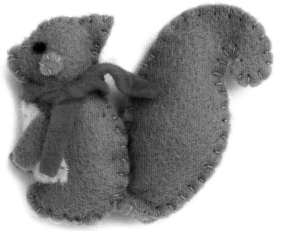

TEDDY BEAR

Materials

White felt, 6 x 9cm (2⅜ x 3½in)

Red felt, 3 x 3cm (1⅛ x 1⅛in)

Fair skin-colour felt, 3 x 3cm (1⅛ x 1⅛in)

Sky-blue felt, 0.8 x 11cm (¼ x 4¼in)

Small amount of dark brown felt

Cotton thread in white, red and fair skin-colour

Small amount of dark brown fingering (4-ply) yarn or embroidery thread

0.5mm (¼in) gold bell

Toy stuffing

Size

6cm (2⅜in)

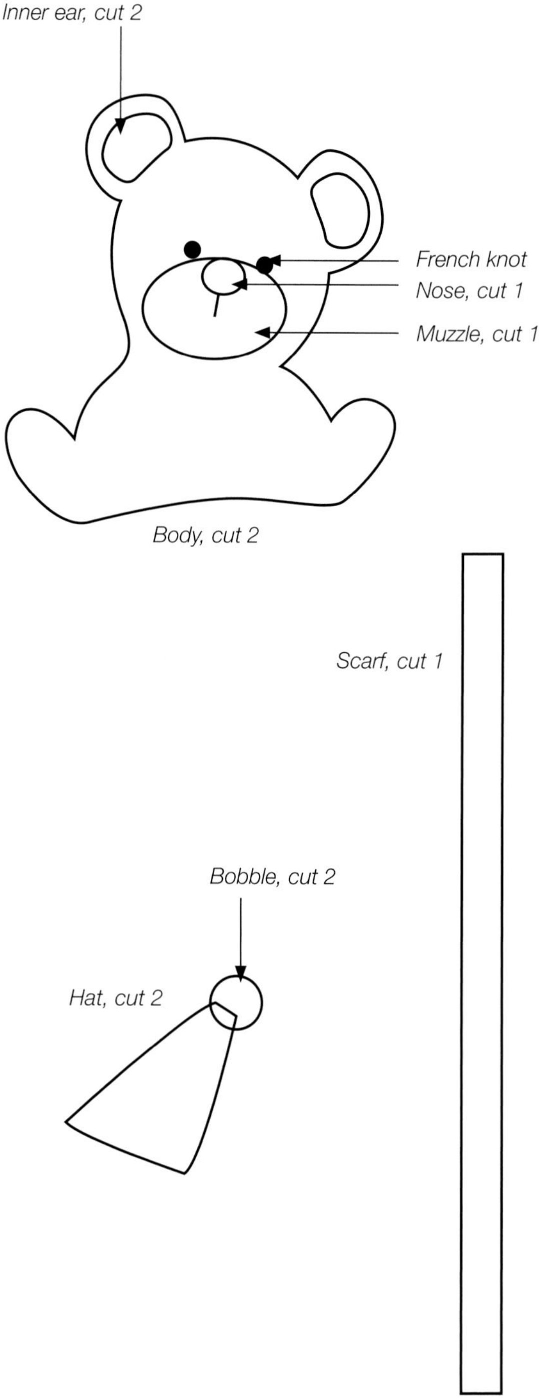

Inner ear, cut 2

French knot

Nose, cut 1

Muzzle, cut 1

Body, cut 2

Scarf, cut 1

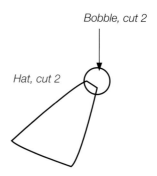

Bobble, cut 2

Hat, cut 2

1 Use the templates to cut out two body pieces in white felt, and two inner ears and one muzzle in fair skin-colour felt. Attach the muzzle and inner ears to the front body piece with fair skin-colour thread and overcast stitches. Cut out a nose in dark brown felt and attach it with dark brown thread and overcast stitches.

2 With fingering (4-ply) dark brown yarn or embroidery thread, French knot eyes and embroider a line to the centre of the nose.

3 Sew the body pieces together with white thread and blanket stitches, stuffing the body as you go.

4 Use the template to cut out two hat pieces in red felt. With red thread, blanket stitch the pieces together, leaving the bottom edge open. Cut out two bobble circles in white thread. Sandwich the tip of the hat with the white circles and using white thread, blanket stitch round the bobble to attach it.

5 Attach the hat to the head with red thread and overcast stitches.

6 Use the template to cut out a scarf in sky-blue felt and tie it round the neck. Attach the bell to the hat with a couple of stitches in white thread.

REINDEER

Materials

Brown felt, 10 x 10cm (4 x 4in)

Small amounts of dark brown, beige and red felt

Cotton thread in brown and beige

Small amount of dark brown fingering (4-ply) yarn or embroidery thread

0.5cm (¼in) gold bell

Toy stuffing

Glue

Size

7cm (2¾in) tall with antlers

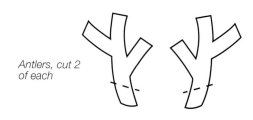

Antlers, cut 2 of each

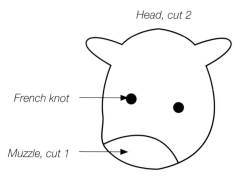

Head, cut 2

French knot

Muzzle, cut 1

Nose, cut 1

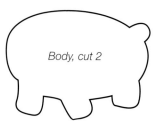

Body, cut 2

Neck ribbon, cut 1

1 Use the template to cut two body pieces in brown felt and sew them together with brown thread and blanket stitches, stuffing as you go.

2 Use the template to cut two head pieces in brown felt and a muzzle piece in beige felt. Sew the top edge of the muzzle piece to the front head piece with beige thread and overcast stitches.

3 With fingering (4-ply) dark brown yarn or embroidery thread, French knot the eyes.

4 Use the template to cut two pieces for each antler and glue the two together.

5 Starting with the bottom right-hand side, sew the head pieces together with brown thread and blanket stitches. Insert the antlers between the front and back head pieces and continue sewing round to secure them (see Brown Bear step 5, page 35). Stop at the edge of the muzzle.

6 Stuff the head. Change to beige thread and blanket stitch the lower muzzle edge, piercing through three layers.

7 Cut the nose from red felt and glue it on. Sew the head to the body using ladder stitch (see the Angel, page 59).

8 Cut a scarf from red felt and tie it round the neck. Trim it to the desired length. Attach the bell to the neck.

OWL

Materials

Dark brown felt, 6 x 9cm (2⅜ x 3½in)

Brown felt, 3 x 6cm (1⅛ x 2⅜in)

Cream felt, 2 x 3cm (¾ x 1⅛in)

White felt, 2 x 3cm (¾ x 1⅛in)

Small amount of yellow felt

Small amounts of black and brown fingering (4-ply) yarn or embroidery thread

Cotton threads to match felt colours

Toy stuffing

Size

5cm (2in)

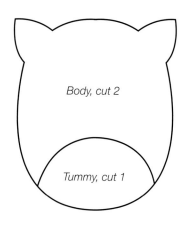

Body, cut 2

Tummy, cut 1

Eyes, cut 2

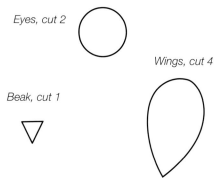

Wings, cut 4

Beak, cut 1

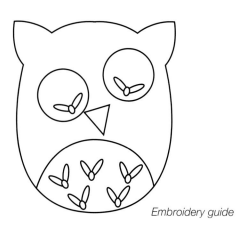

Embroidery guide

1 Use the template to cut two body pieces in dark brown felt and two eyes in white felt. Attach the eyes to the front body piece with white thread and overcast stitches.

2 Use the template to cut one tummy piece in cream felt and attach the upper edge to the body with cream thread and overcast stitches.

3 Cut out a beak in yellow felt and attach it with yellow thread and overcast stitches.

4 With fingering (4-ply) black yarn or embroidery thread, embroider eyes, using fly stitch as shown on page 23.

5 With fingering (4-ply) brown or embroidery thread, embroider the tummy with fly stitches. See the embroidery guide opposite.

6 Sew round the whole body with dark brown thread and blanket stitches, stuffing before you close.

7 Use the template to cut out two sets of wings in brown felt. Blanket stitch the two layers together at the edges. Attach the top halves of the wings to the body with overcast stitches.

SNOWMAN

Materials

White felt, 5 x 7cm (2 x 2¾in)

Blue felt, 1 x 11cm (⅜ x 4¼in)

Dark brown felt, 2 x 3cm (¾ x 1⅛in)

Small amounts of orange and pink felt

Cotton thread in white, dark brown and blue

Small amount of dark brown fingering (4-ply) yarn or embroidery thread

Toy stuffing

Glue

Size

6.5cm (2½in)

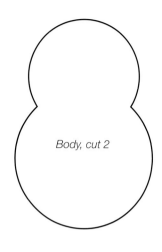

Body, cut 2

Nose, cut 1

Buttons, cut 2

Scarf, cut 1

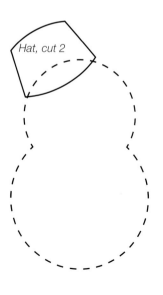

Hat, cut 2

1 Use the template to cut out two body pieces in white felt. With fingering (4-ply) dark brown yarn or embroidery thread, French knot eyes on the front body piece.

2 Sew the two body pieces together with white thread and blanket stitch, stuffing as you go.

3 Use the template to cut two hat pieces from dark brown felt. Sew them together with brown thread and blanket stitch, leaving the bottom edge open.

4 Insert the top of the head into the hat and secure it with dark brown thread and overcast stitches.

5 Use the template to cut out the scarf in blue felt and wrap it round the neck. Secure it to the body with blue thread and overcast stitches.

6 Cut the nose from orange felt and the buttons from pink. Glue them on to the snowman.

GINGERBREAD HOUSE

Materials

Brown felt, 7 x 12cm (2¾ x 4¾in)

White felt, 8 x 9cm (3⅛ x 3½in)

Beige felt, 2.5 x 3cm (1 x 1⅛in)

Small amounts of pink, yellow-green, green, red and sky-blue felt

Cotton thread in white, brown, beige and pink

Toy stuffing

Glue

Size

7cm (2¾in) high

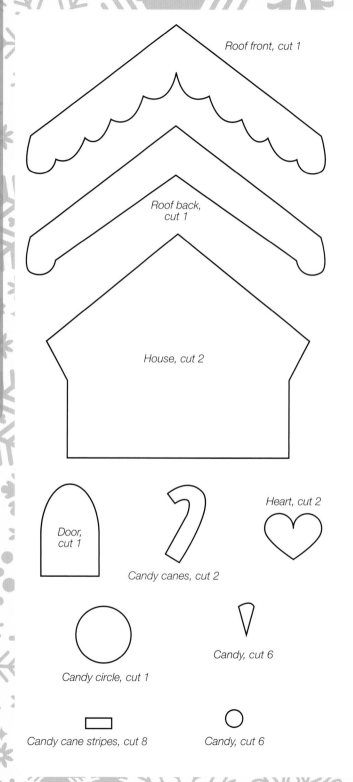

Roof front, cut 1

Roof back, cut 1

House, cut 2

Door, cut 1

Candy canes, cut 2

Heart, cut 2

Candy circle, cut 1

Candy, cut 6

Candy cane stripes, cut 8

Candy, cut 6

1 Use the templates to cut out two house panels in brown felt, and a roof front and back in white felt. Attach the roof front to one house panel and the back to the other with white thread and overcast stitches.

2 Use the template to cut out a door in beige felt and attach it to the house front with beige thread and overcast stitches.

3 Use the templates to cut out two candy canes in white felt and eight stripes in red. Glue the stripes to the candy canes and leave to dry. Cut the excess from the edges.

4 Sew the front and back house panels together with blanket stitches, using matching thread. Stuff the house before closing.

5 Use the templates to cut out a candy circle in white felt and six candies in green. Sew the candy circle to the house front with white thread and overcast stitches. Glue on the candies.

6 Use the templates to cut out circular candies in pink, blue and yellow-green. Glue these on round the door.

7 Use the template to cut out two hearts in pink felt. Sandwich the top tip of the roof with the heart pieces and blanket stitch round the heart with pink thread to secure it.

FOX

Materials

Brown felt, 10 x 10cm (4 x 4in)

White felt, 5 x 5cm (2 x 2in)

Pink felt, 1 x 2cm (⅜ x ¾in)

Pale pink felt, 3 x 4cm (1⅛ x 1½in)

Red felt, 1 x 11cm (⅜ x 4¼in)

Small amount of dark brown felt

Small amount of black fingering (4-ply)
   yarn or embroidery thread

Toy stuffing

Glue

Size

8cm (3⅛in)

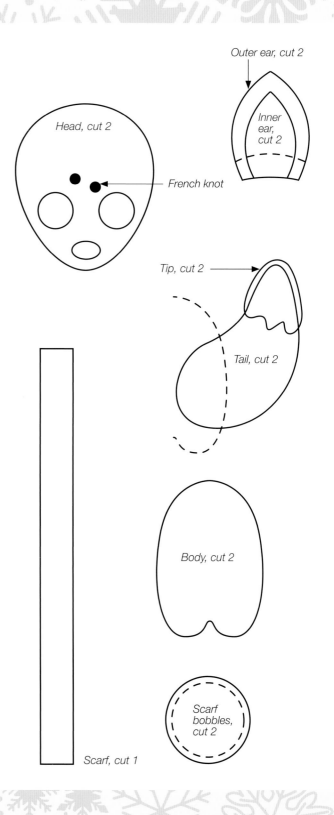

1 Use the template to cut two body pieces from brown felt. Sew them together with brown thread and blanket stitches, stuffing as you go.

2 Use the template to cut out two tail pieces in brown felt and two tail tip pieces in white felt. Sandwich both tail pieces between the white tip pieces and blanket stitch round the tip with white thread. Sew the rest of the tail with brown thread and blanket stitches, stuffing as you go.

3 Use the templates to cut two ear pieces from brown felt and two inner ear pieces from pale pink. Glue the inner ear pieces to the outer ears and leave to dry.

4 Use the template to cut two head pieces from brown felt. With fingering (4-ply) black yarn or embroidery thread, French knot eyes on the front head piece. Sew the head together with brown thread and blanket stitches. Insert the ears when you sew the top edges together (see Brown bear, step 5, page 35). Stuff the head before closing.

5 Use the template to cut out scarf bobbles in white felt. Make the bobbles as for the holly berries for the Candy cane (page 31). Use the template to cut out a scarf in red felt and attach the bobbles. Attach the scarf to the body with a few stitches close to the neck.

6 Attach the head to the body with ladder stitches (see the Angel, page 59). Use the templates to cut out two cheeks in pink felt and a nose in dark brown. Glue them on.

GINGERBREAD MAN

Materials

Brown felt, 5 x 10cm (2 x 4in)

Small amounts of white and beige felt

Cotton thread in brown

Small amount of dark brown fingering (4-ply) yarn or embroidery thread

Cardboard, 6 x 6cm (2⅜ x 2⅜in)

Glue

Size

6cm (2⅜in)

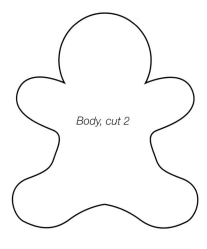

Body, cut 2

Bow, cut 1

Buttons, cut 2

1 Use the template to cut two body pieces from brown felt. With fingering (4-ply) dark brown yarn or embroidery thread, French knot eyes and embroider the mouth with backstitch.

2 Use the same template to cut another body out of cardboard and sandwich it between the felt pieces. Sew all round with brown thread and blanket stitches.

3 Use the templates to cut a bow from white felt and buttons from cream. Glue them on.

Tip

When cutting the body out of cardboard, cut just inside the line to make the filling smaller than the felt pieces.

ELEPHANT

Materials

Grey felt, 10 x 10cm (4 x 4in)

Red felt, 3 x 6cm (1⅛ x 2⅜in)

Grey cotton thread

Small amounts of lilac, pink and yellow embroidery thread

Small amount of black DK (8-ply) yarn

Toy stuffing

Size

9cm (3½in) long

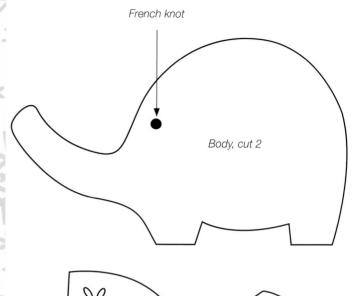

French knot

Body, cut 2

Blanket, cut 2

Ears, cut 2

1 Use the template to cut two blanket pieces in red felt. Embroider backstitch flowers with lilac and pink embroidery thread as shown, making the two pieces mirror images.

2 Use the template to cut two body pieces in grey felt. Sew all round the body with grey cotton thread and blanket stitches, leaving the tummy open. Stuff the body and close the tummy.

3 Sandwich the body between the two blanket pieces. Sew along the elephant's back, using red thread and blanket stitches and piercing through the body to secure the blanket.

4 With yellow embroidery thread and blanket stitches, attach the edges of the blanket to the body.

5 Use the template to cut two ears in grey felt and attach them with blanket stitches.

6 With black yarn, French knot the eyes.

ANGEL

Materials

Cream felt, 5 x 8cm (2 x 3⅛in)

Fair skin-colour felt, 4 x 4cm (1½ x 4½in)

White felt, 4 x 8cm (1½ x 3⅛in)

Yellow felt, 3 x 4cm (1⅛ x 4½in)

Small amounts of fair skin-colour and dark brown fingering (4-ply) yarn or embroidery thread

Cotton thread in fair skin-colour, white, cream and yellow

Toy stuffing

Small amount of gold size 05 pearl cotton embroidery thread

Size

8cm (3⅛in)

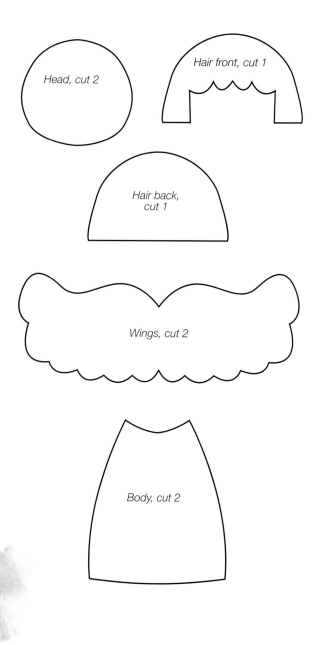

Head, cut 2

Hair front, cut 1

Hair back, cut 1

Wings, cut 2

Body, cut 2

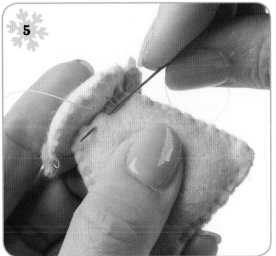

1 Use the template to cut two head pieces in fair skin-colour felt. With fingering (4-ply) fair skin-colour yarn or embroidery thread, French knot the nose on the front head piece. With dark brown, French knot eyes.

2 Use the templates to cut out both hair pieces in yellow felt. Sew the lower edge of the hair front to the face with yellow thread and overcast stitches. Sew round both head pieces with fair skin-colour thread and blanket stitches. Place the hair back piece over the back of the head and use yellow thread to sew the hair pieces together, stuffing the head before closing.

3 Use the template to cut two body pieces in cream felt. Sew them together with cream thread and blanket stitches. Stuff the body before closing.

4 Attach the head to the body with ladder stitches with fair skin-colour thread. First put a stitch in the head as shown above.

5 Next, put a stitch in the body, and continue in this way to sew along the whole width of the body and head.

6 With gold pearl cotton embroidery thread, stitch the halo onto the head using chain stitch. Alternatively, make a 5cm (2in) long chain with a crochet hook. Fasten off and attach the chain to the head.

7 Use the template to cut two wing pieces in white felt. Sew them together with white thread and blanket stitches. There is no need to stuff the wings. Attach to the body with backstitch.

PENGUIN

Materials

Black felt, 5 x 9cm (2 x 3½in)

White felt, 4 x 5cm (1½ x 2in)

Red felt, 3 x 3cm (1⅛ x 1⅛in)

Small amount of yellow felt

Small amount of dark brown fingering (4-ply) yarn or embroidery thread

Cotton thread in white, black, red and yellow

Toy stuffing

Size

6.5cm (2½in)

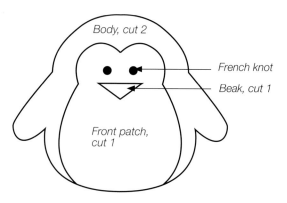

Body, cut 2

French knot

Beak, cut 1

Front patch, cut 1

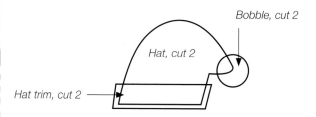

Bobble, cut 2

Hat, cut 2

Hat trim, cut 2

1 Use the templates to cut two body pieces in black felt and one front patch in white felt. Attach the front patch to one body piece with white thread and overcast stitches.

2 Use the template to cut out a beak in yellow felt. Attach it with yellow thread and overcast stitches. With dark brown fingering (4-ply) yarn or embroidery thread, French knot the eyes.

3 Sew the front and back body pieces together with black thread and blanket stitches. Stuff the body before closing.

4 Cut out two hat pieces in red felt and two trims in white. Attach the white trims to the hat pieces with white thread and overcast stitches. Sew the hat together with red thread and blanket stitches. Leave the bottom edge open.

5 Cut two bobble pieces in white felt. Sandwich the tip of the hat in between them and sew round the bobble with white thread and blanket stitches. Attach the hat to the head with white thread and overcast stitches.

CAT IN STOCKING

Materials

Black felt, 7 x 7cm (2¾ x 2¾in)

Red felt, 7 x 8cm (2¾ x 3⅛in)

White felt, 3 x 8cm (1⅛ x 3⅛in)

Small amount of yellow felt

Cotton thread in white, red and black

Glue

Toy stuffing

Size

9cm (3½in)

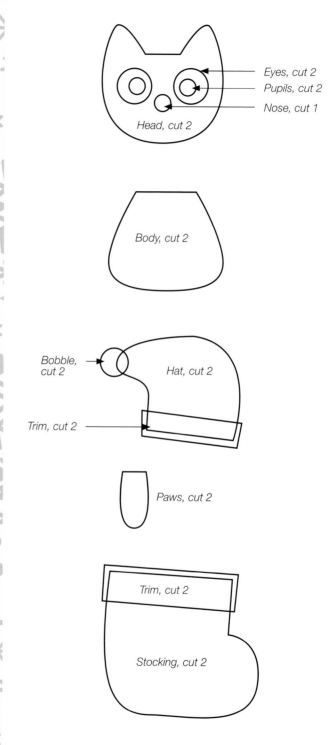

Eyes, cut 2

Pupils, cut 2

Nose, cut 1

Head, cut 2

Body, cut 2

Bobble, cut 2

Hat, cut 2

Trim, cut 2

Paws, cut 2

Trim, cut 2

Stocking, cut 2

1 Use the template to cut out two head pieces and two pupil pieces in black felt, and two eye pieces in white felt. Attach the white eye circles to the face with white thread and overcast stitches. Sew the head pieces together with black thread and blanket stitches. Stuff the head before closing. Glue the pupils to the eyes and leave to dry.

2 Use the template to cut two body pieces in black felt. Sew them together with black thread and blanket stitches. Stuff before closing. Attach the head to the body with ladder stitches in black thread (see the Angel, page 59).

3 Use the templates to cut out two stocking pieces in red felt and two trims in white. Attach a trim to each stocking piece with white thread and overcast stitches. You do not need to stitch the top edge.

4 Sew the stocking panels together with red thread and blanket stitches, leaving the top open. Use white thread to sew up the side edges of the trim.

5 Use the template to cut two hat pieces in red felt and two trims in white, and make the hat in the same way as the stocking.

6 Cut two bobble pieces in white felt and sandwich the tip of the hat between them. Blanket stitch all round the bobble in white thread to attach it.

7 Insert the cat's left ear in the hat and stitch in place with white thread and overcast stitches.

8 Use the template to make two black felt paws. Put the cat in the stocking and attach the paws to the cat's head and to the stocking with black thread and overcast stitches.

9 Glue the pupils to the eyes, and also glue on the nose.

HOLLY WREATH

Materials

Green felt, 6 x 6cm (2⅜ x 2⅜in)

Red felt, 1 x 18cm (⅜ x 7in)

Small amounts of white, sky-blue, yellow and pink felt

Cotton thread in green and red

1cm (⅜in) gold bell

Small amount of lilac size 05 pearl cotton embroidery thread

Toy stuffing

Glue

Size

6cm (2⅜in)

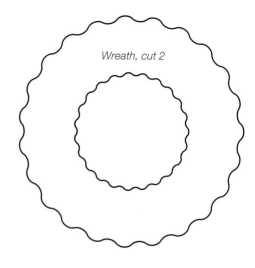

Wreath, cut 2

Ribbon, cut 1

Large bauble, cut 4

Small bauble, cut 4

1 Use the template to cut two wreath pieces in green felt. Lay one on top of the other and and sew the inner edges together with green thread and blanket stitches.

2 Blanket stitch the outer edges together, inserting stuffing as you go.

3 Use the template to cut the ribbon in red felt. Tie it in a bow and trim the tails to the desired length. Stitch the bow to the top of the wreath.

4 Use the templates to cut baubles in the different felt colours and glue on to the wreath.

5 Thread the bell with embroidery thread and attach it to the wreath.

TOY SOLDIER

Materials

Green felt, 4 x 7cm (1½ x 2¾in)

Fair skin-colour felt, 4 x 4cm (1½ x (1½in)

Black felt, 4 x 5cm (1½ x 2in)

Yellow felt, 2 x 3cm (¾ x 1⅛in)

White felt, 1.5 x 8cm (⅝ x 3⅛in)

Cotton thread in fair skin-colour, black, red, white, brown and yellow

Toy stuffing

Small amounts of dark brown, black and fair skin-colour fingering (4-ply) yarn or embroidery thread

Size

9cm (3½in)

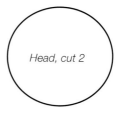

Head, cut 2

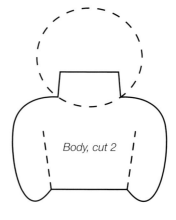

Body, cut 2

Hat, cut 2

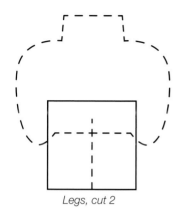

Legs, cut 2

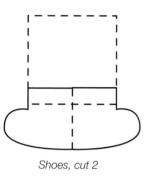

Shoes, cut 2

Epaulettes, cut 2

Bands, cut 2

1 Use the template to cut two shoe pieces in black felt and sew them together at the sides and bottom with black thread and blanket stitches. Leave the top edge open.

2 Use the template to cut two leg pieces in brown felt. Sew the side edges together with brown thread and blanket stitches. Leave the top and bottom edges open.

3 Insert the shoes into the legs and stuff both from the top edge. Secure the trouser hem to the shoes with brown thread and overcast stitches.

4 Pierce through the centre of the shoes with black thread and back stitches to separate them. With brown thread, pierce through the centre of the legs with backstitch to separate them.

5 Use the template to cut two body pieces in red felt. Sew them together with red thread and blanket stitches, leaving the bottom edge open.

6 Stuff the body, insert the legs and secure them to the body with overcast stitches. With red thread, pierce through the body where indicated by dotted lines to create the arms.

7 Use the template to cut two head pieces in fair skin-colour felt. With fair skin-colour fingering (4-ply) yarn or embroidery thread, French knot the nose. With dark brown fingering (4-ply) yarn or embroidery thread, French knot eyes.

8 Sew the head pieces together with fair skin-colour thread and blanket stitches, stuffing as you go.

9 Use the template to cut two hat pieces in black felt. With black thread, blanket stitch them together, leaving the bottom edge open. Insert the head and use overcast stitches to secure it. With black fingering (4-ply) yarn, make long backstitches round the face for straps.

10 Attach the head to the body with ladder stitches as for the Angel (see page 59).

11 Use the template to cut two epaulettes in yellow felt. Attach them at the inner edges of the shoulders with yellow thread and overcast stitches.

12 Use the template to cut two bands in white felt. With white thread, secure them to the body as shown, making overcast stitches at both ends.

SANTA GIRL

Materials

Red felt, 6 x 8cm (2⅜ x 3⅛in)

Fair skin-colour felt, 5 x 5cm (2 x 2in)

Black felt, 2 x 5cm (¾ x 2in)

White felt, 3 x 9cm (1⅛ x 3½in)

Cotton thread in fair skin-colour, black, red and white

Toy stuffing

Small amounts of dark brown, fair skin-colour and red fingering (4-ply) yarn or embroidery thread

Small amount of light brown fingering (4-ply) yarn

Small amount of chunky white fleecy yarn

Size

9cm (3½in)

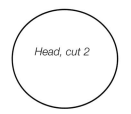

Head, cut 2

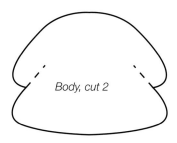

Body, cut 2

Body trim, cut 2

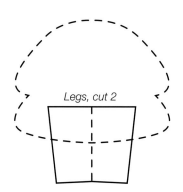

Legs, cut 2

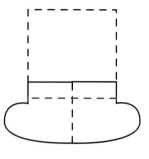

Shoes, cut 2

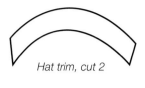

Hat trim, cut 2

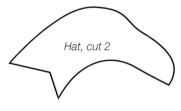

Hat, cut 2

1 Use the templates to cut out the legs in fair skin-colour felt and the shoes in black. Follow steps 1–3 for the Elf on pages 38–39 to make the legs and feet.

2 Use the templates to cut out two body pieces in red felt and two trims in white. Attach the trims to the body pieces with white thread.

3 Sew the body pieces together with red thread and blanket stitches, leaving the trimmed bottom edge open. Stuff the body, insert the legs and stitch the legs and body together with white thread and overcast stitches.

4 With red thread, pierce through the body where indicated in dotted lines on the template to create the arms.

5 Use the templates to cut out two hat pieces in red felt and two hat trims in white. With white thread, attach the trims to the bottom of the hat pieces, using overcast stitches at the top edge and blanket stitch at the side and bottom edges.

6 Use the template to cut out two head pieces in fair skin-colour felt. With fair skin-colour fingering (4-ply) yarn or embroidery thread, French knot the nose. With dark brown fingering (4-ply) yarn or embroidery thread, French knot eyes. Sew the head pieces together with fair skin-colour thread and blanket stitches. Stuff the head and close the seam.

7 With a few strands of fingering (4-ply) light brown yarn, make plaits and secure the ends with red fingering (4-ply) yarn or embroidery thread. Attach the plaits to the head.

8 With the same yarn, make stitches on the forehead, leaving loops every other stitch. Cut the loops to create a fringe and trim.

9 Sandwich the head between the sides of the hat as shown. With red thread, blanket stitch the red part of the hat together. Secure the hat to the head with overcast stitches at the edge of the trim.

10 Attach the head to the body as for the Angel (see page 59). Wrap the neck with white fleecy yarn to make a scarf.

SANTA

Materials

Red felt, 8 x 10cm (3⅛ x 4in)

White felt, 5 x 5cm (2 x 2in)

Fair skin-colour felt, 4 x 4cm (1½ x 1½in)

Brown felt, 3 x 4cm (1⅛ x 1½in)

Cotton thread in red, white, fair skin-
colour and brown

Small amount of dark brown fingering
(4-ply) yarn or embroidery thread

Toy stuffing

Glue

Size

9cm (3½in)

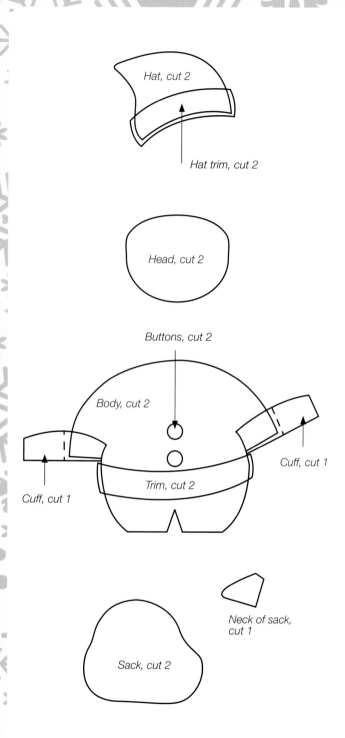

Hat, cut 2

Hat trim, cut 2

Head, cut 2

Buttons, cut 2

Body, cut 2

Cuff, cut 1

Cuff, cut 1

Trim, cut 2

Neck of sack,
cut 1

Sack, cut 2

Beard, cut 1

Nose, cut 1

Shoes, cut 2

Hands, cut 2

Positioning of shoes

1 Use the templates to cut out two body pieces in red felt, then two trim pieces in white felt. Sew the trims to the body pieces with white thread and overcast stitches.

2 Use the templates to cut two shoe pieces in black felt. Fold each piece in half and blanket stitch round the edges, stuffing as you go.

3 Sandwich a shoe inside a leg piece of the body and stitch it to the body with red thread and overcast stitches. Repeat for the other shoe.

4 Use the template to cut out two hand pieces in fair skin-colour felt. Fold each one in half horizontally and blanket stitch round the edges with fair skin-colour thread.

5 Sandwich a hand inside the arm of the body pieces and stitch the hand to the body with red thread and overcast stitches.

6 Blanket stitch round the body with red thread, stuff and close.

7 Use the template to cut two cuffs from white felt. Wrap the wrist with the cuff and stitch it to the body with white thread and overcast stitches. Repeat for the other wrist.

8 Use the template to cut two head pieces, one in fair skin-colour for the face and one in white. Cut one beard in white felt. Stitch the beard to the face with white thread and overcast stitches. Use the template to cut a nose in fair skin-colour felt and stitch it to the face with fair skin-colour thread and overcast stitches. With dark brown fingering (4-ply) yarn or embroidery thread, French knot the eyes.

9 Blanket stitch the face to the white head piece with fair skin-colour thread, stuffing as you go.

10 Use the templates to cut two hat pieces in red felt and two trims in white felt. Attach the trims to the hat pieces with white thread and overcast stitches. Sew the hat together with red thread and blanket stitches, leaving the bottom edge open.

11 Sew the hat to the head with white thread and overcast stitches at the edge of the trim.

12 Attach the head to the body as for the Angel on page 59.

13 Use the templates to cut two sack pieces and one neck of sack piece from brown felt. Sew the sack pieces together with brown thread and blanket stitches, stuffing as you go. Attach the sack to the back of Santa's hand.

14 Sew the neck over the sack over Santa's right hand. Cut out two buttons in white felt and glue them on.